RUNNING LIKE A WOMAN WITH HER HAIR ON FIRE

Running Like A Woman With Her Hair On Fire

Poems

Martina Reisz Newberry

Red Hen Press 🐔 Los Angeles

Running Like A Woman With Her Hair On Fire

Cover art: by Kirsten Brix Jacobvitz, from the private collection of
Eugenie Brix

Book and cover design by Michael Vukadinovich

ISBN 1-59709-015-8

Library of Congress Catalog Card Number 2004117571

Published by Red Hen Press

The City of Los Angeles Cultural Affairs Department, California Arts
Council, Los Angeles County Arts Commission and National Endowment
for the Arts partially support Red Hen Press.

First edition

CONTENTS

For Brian
         . . . plus qu'hier, moins que demain

For Chris and Vanessa
         My smiles, my heart

For Larry Kramer and Rod Santos
         For believing

It's not what you thought when you first began it . . .
It's not going to stop 'til you wise up.
         —Aimee Mann
            Wise Up

When I first saw your gallery
I liked the ones of ladies
But now their faces follow me
And all their eyes look shady.
         —Joni Mitchell
            The Gallery

Expatriation: three girls,
children really, running—not looking back.
One thinks of tidying her room.
One thinks of a grilled cheese sandwich.
The third thinks of the boy back there
in the trees, of his hands, his moans
extinguishing the bird sounds.
"Run!" she screams to those two behind her.
"Run faster. Don't look behind you."
Which one was I?
Which one were you?
That evening, remembering, you said,
"Don't forget. We promised never to tell."

Tell me something covert—even if it's a lie.
Tell me: where you were when John Kennedy's ear blew off.
Tell me: how you observed the place of your lost gods.
Tell me: who you were in bed with then? Was he/she living in
          your eyes, your throat?
Tell me: what were your darkest impulses in those days?
          What did you make stronger and what did you endure?
          Were you ready then, as in the wind of your daughter's hands,
          your son's laughter, for the difficult contours of this earth?

The phone rings and rings in this empty room.
I will never regret not answering it.
Did you wish to be broken?
Did I?

THE ORCHARD

We visited Aunt at her house with the
cement porch and the acre of apricot trees.
Our mothers and fathers said, "Be careful,
stay clean. Aunt said, "Now don't rile the bees."
Cousin Lou, Cousin Pauline, Cousin Craig, and me
wandered as far into those trees as we dared,
then took off our shoes to step on overripe,
fallen fruit. Lou kissed Pauline and dared Craig
to kiss me, but he wouldn't answer the dare,
only led me further into the trees
until we found a clear place to sit where
we could see Lou and Pauline pressing themselves
against each other, mouths open, tongues working.
"They oughtn't," I said, "it's wrong." Cousin Craig
bit his lip and pulled my hair. "Don't worry,"
he said, "it's ok as long as it doesn't
'rile the bees.'" They called us to come back then.
We stared at the sound their voices made.
A fury overtook us as we
started back—a rage. We picked up apricots,
as many as we could, began running,
throwing them everywhere, running with our hands
in the air, shouting and crying out
as if the sky were on fire. "We're here!
We're coming! We're here!"

JOHN, TO THE SEVEN CHURCHES

Write the things which thou hast seen, and the things which are,
and the things which shall be hereafter. Revelation 1:19

I am not doing good work.
Each day, I recede a little further.
I see who I was—standing
on an ice floe (which used to be
the Island of Blue Flowers)—
I wave as I sail away.
"Goodbye!" I shout to myself.
"Bear witness," I call out.
"Tell all who will listen
about the way it used to be.
Tell how the price becomes
dearer and dearer and how
all must run for high ground
because the waters rise
before you know it."
Back on the ice floe,
the woman who was me, nods
and smiles. "I will," she calls back.
"You can count on me."

SOMETHING I AM FEELING NEEDS WORDS

I do not wish to be whole alone
knowing who I am but all by myself;
to say, "Is anyone here?" when I
come home and know
that no one is. I can't revise myself.
I mean, it is a fine thing to know
my own broken branches.
A fine thing. But not alone,
no please, not that. Current thinking
declares my passions null.
All vows are off, it says
you may be cold and cowardly,
but you, by God, know yourself.
Go grab the patent on that one.

A RECKONING

Minds break almost
in the same way a heart does.
It just takes longer.
Even when a heart stops
expecting, stops waiting,
for sleep or peace or the
contrite word, the mind
does not. It stays alert,
on the job. It takes
the photographs, puts forth
the reasonable explanation:
Soon, the mind says, *when
he has rested, when it is
cooler, when it is morning...*
The heart has given up
by this time, has broken,
is shattered. But the mind turns
away from its own distraction.
It refuses to notice
the danger: the exposed root,
the shards of glass, the blown fuse.
when, at last, these things are irrefutable,
it breaks. Just like a heart—
almost exactly like a heart.

PRAYING ON ALL FOURS

She is used to being watched so she tosses
her hair and wipes the beads from her upper lip
with the back of her hand. That moment is
sorcery for him. He stands on the sidewalk,
pretends to look for the bus, but cuts his eyes
to her when he can. He sees her spread lotion
on her shoulders and arms, wonders if he could
pay her to wrap her tanned legs around him,
wonders who will eat dinner with her tonight.
She smiles at him—caught!—he feels barely tethered
to this earth.

It is 5 pm.

At home, his wife checks pot roast, puts biscuits
in the oven. His favorite meal, she thinks.
When he opens the door he doesn't smile.
"I left my briefcase on the bus," he says.
Now a candle has lit itself in her throat.
She can think of nothing to say. Nothing.

A YELLOW TRUCK

In those sad, dreary days
when I was a child, I dreamed
a dream—and it was no small feat
to do this—I dreamed a ride
down some highway in a
yellow truck. I drove faster
and faster, looked down at the road
from my open window and heard
It sing to me of the life
it knew I led: *"Rideaway,*
rideaway, you pale Polack child,
while this is still the worst
anguish you know." How little
I sensed then, so didn't listen
while the cheerless tick tock
of those wheels mimicked
"Rideaway, rideaway."

THE WOMAN WHO READ THE BIBLE

She would get out the Bible.
On an afternoon sometimes,
Mother would get it from
the top shelf of the big
mahogany bookcase.
It wasn't faith she was looking for
among the prophets and poets.
Her mind wasn't right at those times.
She craved a louder voice than
those that wailed inside her head
and beat at her ears. It was
a quick stab at heaven
she wanted; thinking how it might go:
how she might turn a gilt-edged
page and a ray of brilliant light
would shoot forth from the words

and Jesus
Jesus would heal her then and there.

I was the little child who
would lead the savior to her.
I sat still as stagnant water while
she read almost inaudibly
those dreadful stories of miracles:
demons driven into a herd
of swine, a few loaves and fishes
feeding five thousand people,
Lazarus waking up from
death and leaving his grave like
some benign Boris Karloff.
My mother's voice bent and
broke. Finally silent,
she waited for God to see us
sitting side by side on the bed,
bathed in purity and
resolution. Almost shy,
she'd bow her head to whisper
"Amen," and get up unredeemed,
put the book away, and start dinner.

Art Film

I think it was Fellini who said
"People are worth more than reality."
I believe that. I am still that pastel
lump, sitting on my Uncle Paul's couch
in nineteen fifty eight, waiting
for the Yea or Nay of his step—the belt
or his steeltown eyes, smiling, creased
with ol' Smooth-As-Silk from a glass.

       When you say bigger than life,
       think of anger, think of pain, think
       bruises like sunsets: blue, purple, orange.

A simple matter of culture shock,
that's one way to look at it; call it
the barter system; neighbors, behind their
curtains traded tongue clucks for the noises
coming from my Uncle's house. In school
a boy from my neighborhood checked out the marks
on my neck. "Cripes!" he hollered. *"You have
hickeys on your neck!"* He ran to tell.

       Reading Sunday comics on the floor. I think:
       Uncle Paul's a better draw-er than this.
       He draws Snoopy on my hand sometimes.

Uncomplicated terrors. I understood the sound
blood makes chasing itself down my straight
white legs. At night, in my bed, someone sobbed, climbed off me,
said "*Clean yourself*" in a voice thick and congealed
as pudding skin. Half-blind, sleep-starved,
I dozed in school, flunked math, and never
knew why the numbers danced in and out
of equations—refused to rest in peace.

       Some believe that victims are participants;
       that trust goes no deeper than the throat.
       Maybe we know when we're asking for grief.

I believe in the promises
that are made when you win the wishbone pull.
We <u>are</u> better than the reality
that traps us. Even dogs know that a man
is only as clean as his last mess
and that's why he keeps rinsing his hands
under the warm water and running uphill
towards the metallic moon and the
once-bitten-twice-shy stars.

My Mirror on the Table There

What it must be to finish each day with
a promise made, kept! Warm eyes and fingers
and breaths to hear—someone says "yes," or "there,"
or "not yet" and then fills us with a haunting.
I have hidden where there were no doors and
let you pilfer me when I was hungry;
it's all right, I was aware of it,
offered myself up as a whisper or
a bruise, smug and sized to fit a place where
temperance never lived. Give me a decade
to set myself apart. I can absorb all:
waves of meritorious conduct, honey
collected in a jar, expectations of
glory—none of it fairly won. I murmur
to you then you to me: "My father, my
brother, my son—not yet. No, not yet"

I Shall Only Look Up and Say . . .

"I shall only look up and say "Who am I then? Tell me that first,
and then, if I like being that person, I'll come up: if not, I'll stay
down here till I'm somebody else."
                    Alice —*Alice's Adventures in Wonderland*

You understand it perfectly:
The most direct route to knowledge
is denial . . . well, skepticism
at least. Flap of the white apron,
toss of the head, and then,
the decision—to come up only
if you like Being. They'll never love you,
you know. Sweetheart, it's not what
you need anyway. D R I N K M E   E A T M E
those are present, but L O V E M E
is not in any of the vials
or cakes in this story.

You approach yourself from every
angle—a nomad in my story.
Your father was a member
of the Garment Workers' Union,
your mother made albondigas
and tortillas every Saturday.
Certainly, that should tether you.
Look up. The hole you fell into
is still a hole. Up at the top,
the opening there steers the sun
onto your not-so-pretty face.
A blessing.

About the Day You Were Born

Straggler, you broke through, but don't think how,
on the day you were born, the weather or
the news in the newspaper or the
television blatting away may have
placed no blessing on who you came to be.

Maybe that day was the day the whale got lost
in the bay outside San Francisco and
150 people put on their
slickers and jackets and went out to help it
find a way back to its birth canyons.

Or perhaps you were born on the day that
poor, sad woman had simply had enough
of being beaten so she set fire to the
bed there where her spouse slept, never fearing
God's wisdom or his own arrogant demise.

It's just one of those things no one thinks
about much. We remember the date, and
sometimes the time of day and sometimes
the name of the hospital, but seldom
do we think, "It was the day they finally

abandoned the rocket pads at Cape
Canaveral," or "It was the same day
of the month that poor Nat Turner was skinned."
You might sit upstairs in the spare room and
look through an old suitcase at photos

and old letters. You might sit in the old
armchair up there nearly letting yourself
go to sleep with those pictures in your lap,
but, even with all of that, you won't say,
"I was born on the day that crazy

mimosa tree finally bloomed for the very
first time." You won't say it because the only
thing that really feels important is that you
were born, and the changes in the universe
are an entirely different thing indeed.

JAMES DEAN'S SHADOW

My father used to say: *Not everyone casts a shadow.*
I believed it was one of those things adults say; one of
those things only deciphered after you reach thirty and
are allowed to understand everything. You've heard
A-Wink-Is-As-Good-As-A-Nod-To-A-Blind-Horse?
At 56, I'm still not sure what that means.
But shadows...shadows are different. Nobody talks about them.
Though they are faithful, staying with the guy that brought them,
shadows get little attention. This is also true of God.
God is different than he used to be. He notices less now.

Once, it was up to God whether or not you got a shadow,
or kept it once you had it. Now, it's haphazard.
My father had one, so did my favorite uncle. My mother
and her sister each had one. Mother's was long and thin
and preceded her down the hall at bedtime. Aunt Ersta's
was round and mean. You never saw it coming. I am certain
I started out with one, then lost it somewhere and it has
remained lost, unless, of course, it was found by God and
reassigned—the way they reassigned James Dean's shadow
after his horrible car accident. You remember . . .

Triptych

For *Andrew Hudgins*

"*Sweet the nails and sweet the wood, laden with so sweet a load.*"

I. What Was Heard On High

Villagers looked out their windows, leaned way out
over the street and there was Christ Jesus
going by, dead as ever. An altar boy
lifted him in horny hands, ignored
the spring insects—stinging, biting—and Christ Jesus
up there, out of it all. The song moved upward:
"Dulce lignum, dulces clavos, dulce pondus sustinct."
Children stopped eating, lovers stopped loving,
to hear the trumpets, to see the old people
rock side to side, following dear, dead Jesus.

In the windows above the shoe shop, two sisters
spoke in whispers. I saw them: old and lovely,
hair the color of white birches. They put away
the breakfast things and licked the last of the jam
from their fingers and watched the procession:
one of them hummed very sweetly. All around
it was solemn. Even the air swayed.
At night the sisters read to each other from
their father's missal and slept in one bed.
They held hands in the dark. I was there and
saw these things. There was little else to do.

II. In the Tent

I liked his homely hat, though he soon removed it
and shed his coat like a molting snake.
We sang a hymn together; it seemed
to place us on the first rung of a ladder
and the preacher's voice stretched around that tent—
a melodious clothesline hung with bleached underthings.
Souls stayed at Mean Low Water until he
unbuttoned his sleeve cuffs and called us down
so we could show what we were made of. I think
he hoped it was Love, because, when his hands gripped
my head, the fingers quavered in my hair like
old voices praising the cross: "Crux Fidelis."
My sins were deeply buried, redemption
was tentative and hewn out of failure.
On my knees at his feet, I whispered, *"Where
are we going?"*   TO BE SAVED was the answer.

III. Prayers

The complaining prayers are the ones I love:
"What did I ever do to you, Lord?
What did any of us ever do to you?"
There are answers to that. I love the prayers
of the midnight faithful, the ones that quicken my heart,
bring saliva to my mouth in the black
quiet of some robust evening.
"*O God! O Yes, yes. . . God!*" Indicating,
not the acceptance of glory, but a celebration
of vandalism, warm and ripe.

Children vandalize each other's bodies,
not loving until the damage is done,
not understanding that decay will
take over when affection goes to God.
Our abandonment by the saints is less
terrifying than was prophesied
and the Christ Jesus of the stone streets
stopped his ransom attempts years ago.
Now he asks only that we return to Babylon
when our visits to Jerusalem are over.

KISS OF THE VAMPIRE

In the movie, everything is in shades of gray
so that we understand about love being alive
even among the dead. Definitely a gray area.

When he takes her in his arms and she lets him
hold her like this and like this and then
he learns to like it that she worries about

his health and if he's taking his vitamins,
then the scary part really begins. I mean,
as long as he's just love-nipping her

on the throat and lips, it's okay,
but you know and I know—o god yes—we know
that she hasn't the faintest idea,

the foggiest notion, that this will be
the last love of her whole life.
She can't know that,

or she'd never ever ever do it.
Isn't that so?
Isn't it?

Thinking About What Might Happen

You thought about what might happen:
Contemplation of the Wheel—A Portrait
(You were framed.)
We went to buy books; your hands were busy
touching titles as if they were Braille.
Poetry by Touch, a nice concept.
Your mouth was set as if for chocolates
or custard. Consider what was done:
how you smoothed the pages and your fingers
moved, danced—fast as coyotes over
the words. What if. . .what if. . . what if I
had been a whore and not who you know
at all? What if my name was Babylon
and I pulled sentences over my legs
like stockings?
Ah! Bow your head now—hope that, this once,
the night won't be dark.

In A Terrible Country

I seldom say prayers, preferring the off-hand plea
to whatever/whoever might be listening.

I get on my knees to Love's generosity,
or Faith's endurance. Tonight though, I looked for

deities in the river; a goddess, a god,
anyone who might listen and be generous.

Tonight, I called on those spirits I do not love,
asking that you have a change of mind and can see

that I am more than your middle-age woman,
more than my failing eyesight and more than

the blown apart life that has tracked me here.
I have seen water jumping between stones

where the deer come to drink and have wished for things
too terrible to tell. If you could only stand

where I have stood, raging at the tales played
back too often. If you could bury yourself, as I have,

in the year's first full moon and know how an injured word longs
to leap from a burned tongue, then you would be whole,

ready to spread yourself across the landscape
and cry out, blood racing, *This is not enough!*

On the First Day of October

When I learned to tie my shoes,
I always stopped at the same place.
You know that place where the lace
goes around itself, right before the bow
is born. I always stopped right there,
frozen. Time went nowhere, birds stopped
flying, dogs stopped scratching. It was
like a photograph of a bicycle rider—
you can see that he should be moving,
but the picture has caught him in the place
he will be forever: one knee raised, ready
to push down on the pedal.

There is so much one needs to go on through
to all that is waiting. In the case of
shoelace tying, it is courage; in the case
of bicycle riding, it is coordination;
in the case of loving, it is vision.
I once left a friend in San Rafael
who wrote to me. She said: "*I can't believe
how small I have become. I have been
reduced by events, surprised, hurt without
reason, artfully carved up.*"

I don't know. . . check with me later
for the things you need to know.
We can talk about them sometime
when the coffee is poured and too hot to drink;
maybe on the first day of October
when we find just the smallest bit of ice
on the car windshield.

THE RIVER KNEW

I tell you now, that river has answers.
Walk with me? it asked. I did. Listen! it said
I did. And we talked, the water and I,
about a dream I had in which
some large dark birds flew over
my head; their wings sounded like busses
going by and I woke up frightened.
I told this dream to the river, to the
green scum over part of it and to the wild
grasses and strange tall flowers. "What now?" I asked
them all. "What now?" The river smiled and blinked
its teary eyes. *You dreamed all that it told me.*
You are awake now. Look at the path.
Look at the waxwings. Awake is the only answer.
Yes. Yes.

Something I Know About

You inhale the certain grassy smell,
note the towel blowing soft on the line.

"Yes," you nod, *"it will be clear today;*
and there is the cat and there an owl."

You clearly understand, for the moment,
how things are. But, inside, where your hunger sits,

are vital sounds wicked as meteors.
Each small thing competes for its own realness:

A child hugs himself to sleep, a snake
naps in the warm roadway, some tall creature

bends to come in your door,
and, subtler than waking from a nap,

you will go back to where you began,
disposed toward another way of loving.

A Chill Over the Water

The ocean is ruled by the moon.
Not language, not telescopes,
the cool moon. I carry that with me,
say it like an olivewood rosary
over and over, while the watery light
gives my words away.

When will we dance last?
Where is there a bed for us?
These are the songs of ice-bound boats;
they need my protection. I hold them
in my hands—children:
abandoned and dancing.

I have bought stationery to write to you.
It is off-white and sturdy.
"All is well," I will write.
"The weather is cool and damp.
David is well. The children are well.
The dog is too fat, the cat getting old."

I can write such words and know
that something in you will stir;
something in you will look up
and itch and move.
Your blue owl-y eyes will open wide
and your fine fingered hands will close

tight on themselves. "Damn," you'll say.
You will look up at the moon.
"Damn!" and you might pace, playing
with your cigarette, blowing the smoke
through your nose. Do you remember our waltz?
A woman's waltz in a woman's kitchen—

the wine red and staining our tongues and laughter
washing the garlic off my hands?
We sing the songs of ice-bound boats, Friend.
Small wonder that we seem not to find the secrets.
They're all from a warmer climate than we know.
We hop up and down, waving our shirts as flags,

watching the tankers float by without
so much as a blowing of their great horns.
Sometimes we shout "Help!" Sometimes, "Keep going!"
There's not so much as a lone seaman on their decks
to shout back or blow kisses,
or point meaningfully to the ocean, then to the moon.

Still we shout, waving our shirts as flags,
staving off starvation with our talk.

You Can Never Be Sure

It may be the tender turning
of this most fragile of planets,
or some bird's awful cry

so far away you can nearly
not hear it. The Possible
may change to the Impossible

right before your eyes.
I watched a field mouse run
like crazy from my garage,

(from inside the sack of birdseed,
I reckon), across the lawn
toward the bushes. He never made it.

A hawk got him mid-run.
Dying ruins everything,
and not just for field mice.

When I think of this, I am scattered
like hailstones. There are too many
possibilities, none with scientific

underpinnings. When I think of this,
just the very moves: the walk
to our pigeon house with the white

seed bucket; to sit on the linoleum
and make warm noises back at
the feather-footed birds;

to offer their breakfast on
the backs of my hands,
my lower lip, my crossed legs—

all this tells me it is too late
for warnings and I must make
my decisions now.

Untitled

I saw redemption in the revisions of my life.
That's how I saw it. A friend died;
a friend got married; a friend
moved away; I traveled. The truth is
redemption was only
hanging on to the vestiges
of what used to be the heart in me.

A millwright's daughter, body of flaws,
bemused by all the shapeshifting
going on, I looked into
the dark and saw—what? Maybe the magic
of a moonlit floor where I stood
watching a spider find its way
around the shadow of our
Italian Cypress; maybe
the rhythmic architecture
of consolation when I had
no real grief to contend with.

I've been thinking of a song
not contrived, not prolonged—a song,
nonetheless, to outline
the inevitable losses.
I've wanted to be unique,
a woman to make a mockery
of consequences. I've wanted
to be the target of an obsession,
the object of a delicate
balance between a dream not
yet tangible and a ripened wish.
I've wanted to know, Best Beloved,
in the lush rituals of my best self,
what the celebration is about;
what dies and what lasts forever.

THE RAIN, THE RIVER

It rained all morning into the
Los Angeles River and the Pacific
Coast Highway and onto the old road
I take to the post office. By afternoon,
my roof leaked and the carpet smelled like the dog's bed.

The rain was not so mean early on, dusk
brought out its unkindness. Dusk has never
been trustworthy, poor-postured elderly
thing, making its way to dark. It's the infirmity
I hate; the giving in to the day's wheezings.

Twilight brings existence into focus
with the delicacy of a jackhammer.
Of course, I have not believed in reality.
It changes oftener than my world of choice.
Because of this, I can be friends with those

souls in psychiatric confines. Their dreams
are secure whether they are of demons
or the divine. Once, talking with a madwoman
(whose husband had left her after their children
had burned dead in a Christmas fire), I bade her

be resolute and get well. "Ah!" she said,
"Not if it means making car payments.
I think not." She had something there, all right.
I had not yet been born when the day was
divided up into well and unwell.

But, given a say, I would have done away
with twilight. Incessant, this movement toward night,
and these are babyish contradictions.
But, I am edging toward something that will not
be explained: a blessing, a blessing.

HEARST BEACH

Walk as far as this small beach will take you,
to the end, to the warehouses; weathered
wood, blackened and holding back what they've seen.
Light plays there on splintered floors, ridicules
the broken windows and lets the ocean voice
sing through. Leave the sand behind you and climb
the stairs; they'll forgive your trespass. Shipload
after shipload was entertained at their doors.
Men worked here, raged and lifted, pushed against
packing crates, going home only when the holds
were empty and the holdings caged. Here are the
leavings of those whose hardened hands and
sympathies were the same. Withered warehouse
champions, fury long spent in these dirty,
sand-swept temples. They watch, they hunker and watch,
those who kept the cold waters to their promises.
Later, go back down to the sand the way
you came. Go back to your lunch and the gulls
and the rocks. Though you will be asked again and again,
you might never tell what has touched you and where.

Immutable Truths

When I went to see the fortune teller,
I asked questions about my marriage,

the failed crumbs of a banquet coupling.
It was in the afternoon — after lunch —

and my stomach would not stop protesting
the Chinese pork and rice. "Your stomach

knows I'm right," she told me and finished
reading the runes then turned to her cards.

Her eyes squinted and played with the pictures.
"That's it," she said finally. "Nothing else there,"

she shook her head, "unless you got twenty
more dollars." The cards shifted under her

fingers, made a pile, stood silent as God.
Without twenty more dollars to coax

the reluctant future, there'd be
"nothing else there." I told her I guessed not,

slipped my heel back into my shoe and
got back to work an hour late.

It doesn't take a fortune to convince
the spirits to do what they ought to do

for free, but I didn't have twenty dollars
and my husband left me anyway.

POLITICALLY CORRECT IN AMERICA

I told my first husband I wanted
to be kidnapped by terrorists. I would
fall in love with one of them, I said,
and commit terrible political
acts for him like Patty Hearst who really
did it all for love which she called "brainwashing."
My husband took it very personal

though I didn't mean it exactly like that.
His disappointment was evident.
I was insane then, always with my rear
end on one side of the crazy line
and my feet over on the other.
He left me shortly after the terrorist
remark, for a woman who had her degree

in biology and a bank account
of four figures. It was forseeable.
My daughter said I handled it well.
In March, they turned off my lights for the first time.
I borrowed to turn them back on. Then, they
turned off my gas and water. I slept with
a neighbor for money to turn them back on.

Yesterday, the man from the phone company
tried to get into my pants. I've forgotten
his name, but I had the phone turned off because
I can't pay the bill and there was sure as hell
no chemistry between the telephone man
and me. My daughter says "What's the difference?"
I wish I had my degree in biology

and a big bank balance. I wish I knew
how to get those things without maybe
fucking a banker or a few professors.
My paycheck doesn't cover what two
paychecks did and, each time I hear a knock
at the door, I know that the terrorists
are ready for me.

BLAM IN GILEAD

Clearly he had forgotten.
I smell like lilacs, I said,
like sandalwood. His memory
faltered, disturbed by static
and half visions. *I am full
of your sunsets,* I said.

*I am your navigator,
your blazing place.* He drew
a blank on that one. There was
wonder, but no recognition
in his face. *Think of
a picnic,* I told him, *with ants
and rain clouds and the white wine*

turned warm and the croissants soggy.
He shook his fair head. We were
not in Rotterdam or Paris.
A small tremor burst from
the San Andreas Fault.
The lamp and the mirror trembled.

I saw myself in the glass.
I am your Beautiful Loser
I said. His eyes threw sparks
all over the room.
He embraced me and cried.
"I KNEW YOU'D COME BACK."
He just kept saying that.

Things I Thought of Today in the Shower

I prefer my shadow to my reflection,
a sketch of me rather than a photograph;
I'd rather a watercolor wash than a mirror image.
It's just the way I am.

I am interested in the idea of "the Rapture,"
a second chance for the world which, while it may
seem bleak, could work as lye does on olives:
purifying to make worthy.

I used to think I'd live near the ocean, it seemed
important for many years. Then, that desire
became an antique and went another direction–
I wonder who wants it now.

Marilyn Hacker says that, one day, women will
"break our fetters and raise our daughters
to be Lesbians." She sounds angry. Who isn't?
This moment the only moment...

This moment, this Now that no one shares
with anyone is all we have. I am tired
of lessons, tired of learning, tired
of changes, tired of being fat.

If it goes on sale, I'll buy this soap again.

WHEN YOU SAW HER, YOU KNEW . . .

she was the girl with the dark, curled hair
and the red wool coat. She was the girl
the boys chased and waited, impatient, to
push her on the swings.

She was the cheerleader with red hair
who got nine invitations to the
Hawaiian Dreams Dance, the girl who
would not say "hello" to you though she lived
only 2 houses down on your side of the street.

She was the blond in your German class who
never cracked a book and the tiny girl
in your Theater class whose black eyes
burned the boys to ash.

She was the brunette in your office
who wore micro-mini skirts, who fluttered
scarlet-tipped nails and never
had to pay for her own lunch.

You knew who she was the moment
your husband introduced her
and you knew—saw—the way
he smiled at her, saw the axe in his hand.

BILL'S CHRISTMAS CARD: 1967

Don't count me out yet, you said and then wrote
of the geese you saw leaving in September.

You moved slowly, even before your illness,
so I hardly noticed a difference until

your right foot pointed inward with pain;
a strange phenomenon, I thought. You smiled

spoke of a cramp and then told me the news.
I barely recall the day except for

your hair-a bright penny topping your white
face. You said you were not really so sick;

you would trick the doctors and God and your
ex-wife and your bill collectors and the odds.

From a last hospice in Vermont, your card:
Don't count me out yet. I have a farewell

for you, saved for the holidays. A book
of drawings: the moon and the sea, a red

tree, rain on some street, coins on a shelf,
three children running, ice patterns on the street.

It is acceptance we're after. Somewhere
outside this room, you open your eyes, rise

and wait for the morning's first cigarette,
the sound of a bell far, far across town.

THE DISMORPHIA BUTTERFLY:
  PROTECTIVE MIMCRY IN A SINGLE SPECIES

We had to show all things in the only light
there was. We might have bought that farm, hoping
to conjure up a tethering spell, holding what
was between us fast between us. Those were days
of driftwood courage-everything terrible and
beautiful. I used to be brave.
As brave men die, I died, my courage keeping
its vows in windroar and in dark arcades.

Perhaps I am a redneck farmwife business
as usual my only beauty a perfect
piecrust every time. Well, it is a holy
strangeness, a pretend,
the cold weight of pale water.
You could be an osprey and I could be
honey in your mouth.
What is your pleasure?
        "Whisper it. What is your pleasure?
Surely not remorse. the only remorse here
lives in salt creeks and birch groves;
the crane and the catbird sing its praises.

Now we have the morning.
It flows into us to be gathered,
grasped, then me. What is your pleasure?
Whisper it.
                                Gesture.
As for me, sometimes I think about that pace
where I heard the owls and chewed mint, where
everything that meant anything lay under my hands.

ATLAS

For Brian: cartographer, lover, husband

You breathe in the night, slow and quiet:
once for me and once for yourself then catch
your breath, hoarding it like silver. Your feet
are warm against my legs. In summer
the dark is too hot and close and there is
such stillness...spidery dreams that stretch over
us like an unfinished argument.
Outside it is too quiet. even
the crickets sweat and sound cranky. Cats tango
on our trash can lids-foreplay, then angry
lovemaking then more dancing while I
listen and laugh and sleep again on sheets
like relief maps of distant countries.
In this dark, I am a light to no one
but myself. Somewhere a nightmare finds me;
you wake me up to talk a little and
it is almost as though a rainfall has begun.

WITH THE KOI
    For my Father

In the long afternoons
I sometimes dream of you, Dad,

so tall-a child's lie-rattling
the pages of your newspaper.

Your glasses glint, your eyes
strain white, then I wake.

You did not know, that morning,
how the students were cleaning

the Koi pond and found
at the bottom what looked like

a human hand. They walked down
with buckets and brushes

and fine clean intentions to drain
the Koi pond and scrub its sides.

That's when they found it; just after
the pond was drained, the Koi afraid.

In the evening, the nurse called
to say, "Hurry, your father

is dying." And I began
to move like Esther Williams

in a water ballet, like
a piscean ballerina—

selfish and keen and beautiful
in my reluctance. One student

laughed; another, they say
vomited, but the one

who fished it out,
a tiny Vietnamese girl

studying civil Engineering,
only pursed her lips and sniffed

and suggested they get on with it.
I'm grateful, Dad, that you were not Catholic,

had a priest been there, I swear
I would have cried to offer him

the usual thing. Instead,
I touched your dry hand, stood

a while to harbor...something
for your emptied self.

At the Yellow Cafe

Everything that had a right to
was blooming. My wildflower garden
was a copy of your own, looked like
a magazine photo. You said we
should meet so I chose a new skirt
and wore my hair down. We had coffees
at the Yellow Café and through
the bitter steam, I could smell death
all over you like too much
after shave lotion. I wanted you
to myself, didn't know you would bring
a stranger, her long name all
she needed to take you from me.
("Howdy do. I'm Myasthenia Gravis.

Happy to make your acquaintance.")
Bitch. She owned you, stared out at me
through your eyes to tell me so,
her purity of purpose wrapped
soft around you like a down quilt.
You spoiled your women, baptized
yourself in them, out of touch
with me for months, born again
lost in eyes and breasts and legs-
backpacking in the wilderness,
it was like that. Sometimes you came
back from such trips, held me, said
we ought to settle in together
after all. At the Yellow Café,
"Myasthenia" rolled 'round your mouth

like a country singer's name.
I didn't feel sad until the sun
coming in the window got caught
in your beard and stayed there.
In the parking lot, I kissed you
on the mouth, putting tongue in it,
putting an invitation in it,
putting all we knew together
into your mouth from mine. I said
"Call me," and left. Months later,
when someone phoned and said you were dead,
I remembered the poem about
graves running "all the way to the sea"*
and I moved around inside my house
like a phantom ship on a phantom ocean,
blessing what I will never comprehend.

*from "To Lorca" by Lawrence Raab

At the Solstice, Shuddering in My Picture

I am clever. My father said so, my mother
stayed silent and wished that I would take
up sewing. She wanted to give me something

and thought herself too dumb
to give me intelligence. She could, however,
sew, and wanted to give me that.

I refused it, of course, wanted something else:
to watch a vine reach stem-by-leaf up
our California-pink concrete wall and tell of it;

make a victory over language; some way
to watch words turn cartwheels, then die,
then turn them again in another verse.

I wanted to be too smart to cook and too talented
to clean. After all, did anyone ask Bly
to clean up his messes? (They asked Plath

and she did it). I wanted to bounce back from
womanhood into brilliance, from female to wordsmith,
make bloody transcendence a way of life. I was a homely puppy,

believing love would save me, looking up at man after
man, beseeching him "Teach me. Teach me.
I can learn," my legs open, my tail wagging at them all

(until my years began to catch up and my tail lost its
comely twitch due to the ravages of gravity). Such losses
make me a less desirable pupil—a thing I always knew.

A little talent: I have that, they tell me. The occasional sentence
published Here or There, and—many years ago—a little book.
My father died and I was no longer clever.

My mother died and I ought to have been born,
but I was seeking the enemy, thought I knew him,
was bested by him. Desperate now, I believe

that there is no enemy save all that I have not done.
I sit at the typewriter, hands idle on the keys,
I write:

A PLEA TO ANY GOD THAT MIGHT BE PAYING ATTENTION

Please Something,
happen!

Thank you.

XXOO,
Martina

GAY REPARTEE

Sit with me; I want to explain something:
I've always tended to myself, taken care of

my own needs—"only" children are like that.
We get overlooked in the long run

and we do not mind it.
In my stucco house, I read books,

played with make-believe brothers and sisters;
I kept the radio volume low and spoke

when spoken to. There was grace in the world then.
I cultivated a soft voice and a gentle nature.

I learned generosity from a neighbor lady
who shared pomegranates with us.

I learned a cheery outlook from
the Downs Syndrome boy my mother babysat.

I learned how to cook from
the Lebanese woman across the alley.

"What smells good, tastes good," she said.
Believe it. I smell as good as anything

that ever came out of my kitchen.
When I turned 12, a family friend told me I was homely,

said it was time I *learned something about life*,
said no other man would want me, probably,

then bedded and beat me for two years running.
Who knew to tell a grownup? (They don't like surprises.)

"I'm sorry," I said when my mother found out. "I'm sorry,"
I said when my daddy asked why.

A husband put marks on me that turned
my body into a roadmap.

"I'm sorry," I told him, "to have made you so angry.
I'm sorry. I'll try harder to do what you want."

As he was pulling out of the driveway, in our only car,
he said I was the sorriest woman he'd ever known.

I considered how that was probably true. His unkindness
should have made me mean as swamp water,

but, no, I will give you anything that is mine to give.
This is something you know, dear love.

You are so good to look at, my tongue sticks
to the roof of my mouth, I get breathless.

What is it like for you to know that? I trudge ahead
with my best self in my open hands, trusting my

fine qualities to be enough for anyone. They
ought to be, yes? So why, then, do I find myself

living the same apology over and over,
running like a woman with her hair on fire?

TOUGH NUTS

You forget how quiet Quiet is.
You look around at the stacks of books,
on metal shelves—not like the old libraries
with their dark impenetrable woods,
              light coming through small high windows,
              some books placed too high
              for you to reach

Libraries were dark, lamps (amber light)
always lit, librarians' glasses reflecting
your own timidity: "Yes, please, Ma'am,
all five," as you handed her your card.
              "I'll read them all in one day, too."
              Librarians never believed that.
              Tough nuts those women.

This new branch is all metal and glass
and fluorescent lighting. The librarian
wears contact lenses and smiles—
believes what the children tell him.
              You forgot that Quiet and old wood
              go together and it is a fact that
              aluminum-framed windows admit no ghosts.

This new library says, *Speak up! I can't hear you
if you whisper.* It says, *Look around! No unlit corners*
here. No haunted closets. No hands-off ladders for
librarians only. No smell of old paper. No bookbinder tape.
              It says *Computers. Cell phones. Pagers.*
              Stay tuned. They'll all go off at once
              if you wait long enough.

Still, you are here on opening day: Three Best Sellers,
two True Crime, two Poetry, one Collected Letters.
you offer your card. "Three weeks," says the librarian.
"I'll have them read in 5 days," you say proudly.
　　　He glances up. He doesn't believe you.
　　　Outside, you set down your book bag.
　　　and do a victory dance. Ha! Ha!

Spin the Bottle

I brought my face closer
and closer to the mirror—
knew enough not to stick
my puckered-up lips out
too far, knew that wasn't
how they did it in the
movies. So, I kept my
mouth relaxed, my eyes half closed;
I imagined that I
looked like my beautiful
cousin Kate who sometimes
earned money modeling,
or like Natalie Wood—
huge-eyed and sexy.
I pressed my lips, slightly
open (and smeared with
Primrose Pink lipstick),
to my own reflection,
pressed hard, let my tongue rest
on the cool glass then drift
back into my mouth.
I practiced kissing
that same way a million
times when Mother and Dad
were out, until I was
certain that my first real kiss
would be perfect. When it
finally happened at
Beth Quinn's' birthday party
(the Dr. Pepper bottle
pointed straight at me
after Jimmy Titus
spun it), I closed my eyes
and leaned forward, breathless
in the moment. Jimmy
smelled like pretzels and punch.

When he finished pasting
his mouth on mine, we both
wiped our lips on our sleeves
and laughed out loud.

It Was Me

The girl in the sunbonnet
was looking straight into the camera eye,
straight into Mother's face
(who said to me, "I was taking the picture
so of course she was looking
at me" and I thought that was pretty odd
because Mother never took
pictures though she was in a lot of them).
So we turned the pages
of the album one page after another,
but I kept going back to
the sunbonnet girl with her white bread face
shadowed in the hat bill—
bonnet strings in a huge fake-happy bow—
and her eyes concerned. I asked over
and over *but who is that? who is she?*
until finally Mother said,
"Silly, that's your cousin Tish, you should know that."
But it wasn't Tish. It was me

THEOLOGY

The sliver of glass,
the sun so white, it thinks
itself a moon, this haze
that smells of a desert wind:
all these tell that
Fall is here.
They ask
"Are you ready for death?"
My mother said no,
said neither would I be.
I smiled at her. "O," I said
"but you have not seen me
silent as stone, poised,
a tongue of fire over my head—
waiting for the Pentecost."

A CYCLE OF MOVEMENTS

I. EXPOSITION
The woman who bought my piano was
clearly feeling ragged. She called first, mentioned
my ad, then called again to get directions,
then called a third time to change the time she'd come.
My daughter asked, "Are you sad because you
have to sell it?" I told her *Hell no! It
reminds me of bad things.* Then I cried because,
in truth, I was sad to sell it. I was
not in such good shape then. Scared mostly,
losing my mind a little, (not enough,
the shrink told me, to get an off-work notice,)
thinking all the time *I'm having a divorce;
I am now an ex-wife. What's going to happen?*
Selling the piano was one thing about
to happen; paying the light bill with half
the money was another. Sending half
to my ex who insisted it was his,
was still another.

II. Development

Mrs. Lowe, when she got there, sat down
on the piano bench. She touched the keys.
She asked if I had something to drink. *Tea?*
I offered. Coffee? Water? Soda?

                              "I mean drink," she said,
                              "you know…hard liquor."
I got down the vodka and poured her a
shotglass on ice. She drank it right down.
Have you played a long time? I asked her.
                              "I don't play," she said.
Are you buying it for a family member?
                              "No," she said.
Taking a deep breath, I asked, *Are you going*
to buy it?
                              "How much is it?"
One thousand dollars, I told her, *like*
 it said in the ad. Take it or leave it.
                              "I'll take it."
Would you like another drink? I asked her,
grateful to her for buying my piano.

                              "Sure. Bigger this time."
Then the phone rang. "Is there a Mrs. Lowe there?"
I said *Yes.* "May I speak with her?" I said *Yes.*
I gave her the receiver, her fingers
twisted the phone line round. Then she hung up.
                              "I'm leaving now."
Will you be picking up the piano soon?
                              "No. Not the piano."

III. Recapitulation

She put her empty glass on the piano bench,
walked out the front door. I watched her drive off.
When my daughter asked, "Did she buy it?"
I couldn't answer. I wanted to forget
she'd been there. My daughter touched my arm,
"Are you drinking," she asked, "before noon?"
My sad, sweet girl…*She was, I wasn't*, I said,
Man! And I thought I was on the edge…

HER JOURNEY FROM THE CLINIC

to home must have made her tired.
Maybe it was the ride in
the car, maybe her sister
or my father asking
again and again, "Is it
too cold in here? Shall I
close the window? How do you feel?"

All that in a drive of one hour.
When she got out of the car,
wearing the new sweater
she'd knitted at the clinic,
my father took her elbow
and steered her up the driveway
to our living room. She sat

in a wash of exhaustion,
smiling at me as if I
was the only one who could
comprehend the circumstances.
The room was charged with sympathy
and an ecology of
mistrust. There was an ache,

a discomfort in my chest
which I recognized as
accountability and
reconciliation.
And there was, ahead of us,
a bible of new things
to be and do and bow to.

PARADOXES

TWO BOOKS: 1999 *Guide to Literary Agents* on top of
            The Art and Craft of Writing Fiction

AN "*I Love You*" Teddy Bear sitting on
            An Index of Serial Killers

The book I've had the longest:
            a journal never written in.

TWO POSTERS ON MY WALL: Amelia Earhart next to
            Alfred Hitchcock

A SCRAP OF PAPER ON MY BULLETIN BOARD: "Where are you?"
            I don't know who wrote it or where I got it.

A POSTCARD TACKED TO MY DOOR: The *Oriental Fantasy Room* at the
            Madonna Inn—message on back is unreadable.

A SACHET IN MY UNDERWEAR DRAWER—blue, smelling like baby powder—
            a tiny bloodstain on the corner.

A PHOTOGRAPH: of me with my arm around a woman I've never seen before.
            She looks sexy. I do not.

GRASS CLIPPINGS in an envelope with a Polaroid
            of my daughter holding a duck.

A SMALL GOLD PIANO—A CHARM—from somewhere.
            I don't know where.

LATTES

After I had not seen you in a long time,
We met at that coffee place near the bait shop.
You said, "O you look so ...I like your..."
I said, "I got them...you know that shoe store..."

You said, "My mom and dad sold their..."
The waitress said, "Who wants more coffee?"
In the glistening daytime, our hands fluttered,
we recalled that stretch of road in Fremont

where a big-bellied sheriff almost
gave you a ticket. You were respectful,
said "Yessir" to him, and, when we got away,
without trouble, told me you were scared of him.

I didn't believe it at the time, don't now.
I said, "I'm so glad you came." A pause,
then you upended the day—paralyzed it:
"M", you said, "what if all the bridges in

all the world suddenly fell into the water
below them on top of boats and ferries?
What if they all fell at the same time. What
would matter then? *Would* anything matter?"

I thought of my glued-together life:
the contracts I made, the slitted eyes
of the office, my long skirts shuffling through
the halls and studios, my manicured

nails clicking on keys. What were all these
if not bridges? "So what if they did?" I said.
"There would be weeping and wailing and gnashing
of teeth and then, so what?" You nodded.

Silent, we relived the day's meeting.
"This weather is getting old," I said.
"I like you in blue," you said. We looked over
at a young black man just coming in,

his hair in yard-long extensions, rings
on all fingers. And then it was time to go
and we were anxious to return to
what usually kept us from each other.

I drove away, seeing you in the mirror,
As you bent down to look at something
in the gravel of the parking lot.
The sun looked odd, like it was shining through

cheesecloth, and there was a bad taste in my mouth.
Nearly there, I stopped at the side of the road
and threw up. I wiped my lips with tissue,
then drove on over the bridge to home.